POCKET
MAYA ANGELOU
WISDOM

Inspirational quotes and wise words
from a legendary icon

Hardie Grant

BOOKS

contents

maya angelou on...

se

empo

"

If you don't like
something, change it.
If you can't change it,
change your attitude.

"

"

We may encounter many defeats but we must not be defeated.

"

"

I've learnt that people
will forget what you
said, people will forget
what you did, but people
will never forget how
you made them feel.

"

66

It's one of the greatest gifts you can give yourself, to forgive. Forgive everybody.

99

"

The thing to do, it
seems to me, is to
prepare yourself so you
can be a rainbow
in somebody else's cloud.
Somebody who may not
look like you...

may not call God the
same name you call God
– if they call God at all.
I may not dance your
dances or speak
your language. But be
a blessing to somebody.
That's what I think.

99

self-empowerment

66

You may not control
all the events that
happen to you, but you
can decide not to be
reduced by them.

99

"

There is no greater
agony than bearing an
untold story inside you.

"

"

Nothing will work
unless you do.

"

self-empowerment

66

When you learn, teach.
When you get, give.

99

66

If you're always trying to be normal you will never know how amazing you can be.

99

self-empowerment

"

Do the best you can
until you know better.
Then when you know
better, do better.

"

"

Nothing can dim
the light that shines
from within.

"

66

My wish for you is that you continue. Continue to be who and how you are, to astonish a mean world with your acts of kindness. Continue to allow humour to lighten the burden of your tender heart.

99

66

Develop enough courage
so that you can stand
up for yourself and
then stand up for
somebody else.

99

66

It is important that
we learn humility, which
says there was someone
else before who paid
for me.

99

"

I believe probably the
most important single
thing, beyond discipline,
in any artistic work is
to dare.

"

"

One isn't necessarily
born with courage,
but one is born with
potential. Without
courage, we cannot
practise any other virtue
with consistency.
We can't be kind, true,
merciful, generous
or honest.

"

maya angelou on...

Lo

love

66

If we lose love and
self-respect for each
other, this is how
we finally die.

99

love

"

Love recognises no barriers. It jumps hurdles, leaps fences, penetrates walls to arrive at its destination full of hope.

"

love

"

Whatever you want to do, if you want to be great at it, you have to love it and be able to make sacrifices for it.

"

love

"

In the flush of love's
light, we dare be brave.
And suddenly we see
that love costs all we are,
and will ever be. Yet it
is only love which sets
us free.

"

love

"

Everything of value
takes work, particularly
relationships.

"

love

"

The most called-upon
prerequisite of a friend
is an accessible ear.

"

love

66

There is an intimate
laughter to be found
only among friends.

99

love

66

Let the brain go to work,
let it meet the heart,
and you will be able
to forgive.

99

love

66

Yet if we are bold, love
strikes away the chains
of fear from our souls.

99

love

"

Yet it is only love
which sets us free.

"

love

"

I have a belief that if you don't love something, you'll never be great at it.

"

love

"

The desire to reach
the stars is ambitious.
The desire to reach
hearts is wise and
most possible.

"

love

"

We are stronger, kinder,
and more generous
because we live in
an atmosphere where
love exists.

"

66

To those who have given up on love, I say, 'Trust life a little bit'.

99

maya angelou on...

society

and culture

66

A black person grows up
in this country – and in
many places – knowing
that racism will be as
familiar as salt to the
tongue...

also, it can be as
dangerous as too much
salt. I think that you
must struggle for
betterment for yourself
and for everyone.

99

66

Prejudice is a burden
that confuses the past,
threatens the future and
renders the present
inaccessible.

99

66

Hate, it has caused a
lot of problems in the
world, but has not
solved one yet.

99

"

The truth is, no one
of us can be free until
everybody is free.

"

"

I think a hero is any
person really intent on
making this a better
place for all people.

"

"

The ache for home lives
in all of us, the safe
place where we can go
as we are and not be
questioned.

"

"

We are not our brother's keeper; we are our brother and we are our sister. We must look past complexion and see community.

"

"

We must wage ceaseless
battle against the forces
of greed and hatred...

which are the
foundations of all
political inequality.

99

"

Don't be a prisoner
of ignorance...

the world is larger, far
more complicated, and
far more wonderful than
ignorance allows.

99

66

When we unite in
purpose, we are greater
than the sum of our
parts.

99

"

I believe that each of us
comes from the Creator
trailing wisps of glory.

"

66

Elimination of illiteracy is as serious an issue to our history as the abolition of slavery.

99

66

I have found that
among its other benefits,
giving liberates the soul
of the giver.

99

"

Dear Creator, You,
the borderless sea of
substance, we ask you to
give to all the world that
which we need most –
Peace.

"

66

How important it is
for us to recognise
and celebrate our heroes
and she-roes!

99

maya angelou on...

li

life

66

Bitterness is like cancer.
It eats upon the host.
But anger is like fire.
It burns it all clean.

99

life

"

Life loves to be taken
by the lapel and told:
'I'm with you kid.
Let's go.'

"

life

"

If one is lucky, a
solitary fantasy can
totally transform one
million realities.

"

66

You can't use up
creativity. The more
you use, the more
you have.

99

life

"

We delight in the beauty
of the butterfly, but
rarely admit the changes
it has gone through to
achieve that beauty.

"

life

"

When someone shows you who they are, believe them the first time.

"

life

"

Everything in the
universe has a rhythm,
everything dances.

99

"

Do not just teach
because that's all you
can do. Teach because
it's your calling.

"

life

66

Life is pure adventure,
and the sooner we realise
that, the quicker we
will be able to treat
life as art.

99

life

"

Laughter and smiles
are essential factors in
a joyous life.

"

66

Those who would use
ridicule as a form of
humour, sow nothing
but shame and
bitterness...

life

and when the snide
laughter ends, they
will reap only anger
and hostility.

99

life

"

The idea of overcoming
is always fascinating
to me. It's fascinating
because few of us realise
how much energy...

life

we have expended just
to be here today.
I don't think we give
ourselves enough credit
for the overcoming.

99

life

"

One must nurture the
joy in one's life so that
it reaches full bloom.

"

"

I've learnt that you
shouldn't go through life
with a catcher's mitt
on both hands; you need
to be able to throw
something back.

"

maya angelou on...

her

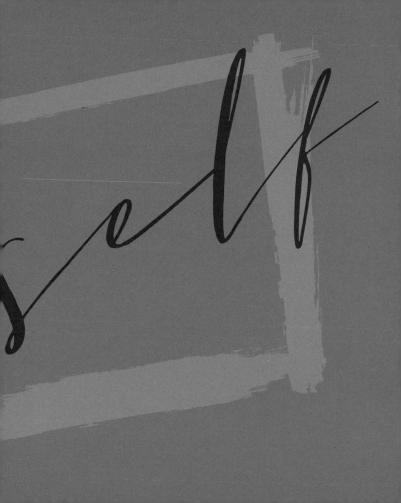

herself

"

I long, as does every
human being, to be
at home wherever
I find myself.

"

"

I am grateful to be a
woman. I must have
done something great
in another life.

"

"

I refuse to allow any
man-made differences to
separate me from any
other human beings.

"

66

I've learnt that whenever
I decide something with
an open heart, I usually
make the right decision.

99

herself

"

I've learnt that I still
have a lot to learn.

"

66

I've learnt that making a
living is not the same
thing as making a life.

99

66

You are the sum total
of everything you've ever
seen, heard, eaten
smelled, been told,
forgot – it's all there...

herself

Everything influences
each of us, and because
of that I try to make
sure that my experiences
are positive.

99

herself

"

I learnt a long time ago
the wisest thing I can do
is be on my own side, be
an advocate for myself
and others like me.

"

herself

"

Let me tell so much
truth. I want to tell
the truth in my work.
The truth will lead
me to the light.

"

herself

"

I always felt, in any
town if you can get to
a library, I'll be OK.
It really helped me as
a child, and that never
left me...

herself

So I have a special place
for every library, in my
heart of hearts.

99

herself

"

My mission in life is
not merely to survive,
but to thrive;
and to do so with
some passion...

herself

some compassion,
some humour, and
some style.

99

herself

"

Energy is like electricity
to me, so when I work,
I try to put myself in
a mood that creates
a friction.

"

"

I respect myself and insist upon it from everybody. And because I do it, I then respect everybody, too.

"

Pocket Maya Angelou Wisdom

Published in 2019 by Hardie Grant Books,
an imprint of Hardie Grant Publishing

Hardie Grant Books (London)
5th & 6th Floors
52–54 Southwark Street
London SE1 1UN

Hardie Grant Books (Melbourne)
Building 1, 658 Church Street
Richmond, Victoria 3121

hardiegrantbooks.com

British Library Cataloguing-in-Publication Data. A catalogue
record for this book is available from the British Library.

ISBN: 978-1-78488-246-4
20 19 18 17 16 15 14 13 12 11

Publishing Director: Kate Pollard
Senior Editor: Molly Ahuja
Junior Editor: Eila Purvis
Design: Jim Green
Cover Illustrator: Michele Rosenthal
Colour Reproduction by p2d
Printed and bound in China by Leo Paper Products Ltd.

FSC
www.fsc.org
MIX
Paper from
responsible sources
FSC™ C020056